The Heartbeat of Humankind

Poems from a Healthcare Worker's Perspective

Ricki Wegner

BookLeaf Publishing

India | USA | UK

Made with ❤ on the BookLeaf Publishing Platform
www.bookleafpub.in
www.bookleafpub.com

To the midwives, nurses, doctors, and all healthcare workers of Afghanistan. Your dedication and courage are an inspiration to the world.

Acknowledgments

Special thanks to the illustrator, Easton Kimball, who made this poetry collection come alive with her beautiful illustrations. And to Farida, who has been with me every step of this publishing journey, as well as the whole team at Bookleaf Publishing. Thank you to everyone who has been a part of my training and growth as a healthcare worker. Special thanks to Melissa, Vicki, Katrina, and Sondria, the Institute for International Medicine (INMED), the Institute of Ultrasound Diagnostics, Mercy in Action, and the National Midwifery Institute. Thank you Megan from @_viablesolutions_ and Marybeth from @sonoeyesultrasound for teaching me so much about fetal heart ultrasound. Thank you, Mom and Dad, for encouraging me to chase my dreams and fostering a deep love for God and people, my siblings for always having my back, and my husband and kids for your love, support, and many amazing adventures together.

Preface

There are certain interactions with patients that I will never forget. Being a healthcare worker is both deeply fulfilling and incredibly challenging. It is an honor to be there for people on the best and worst days of their lives. These moments have stayed with me and have shaped how I see the world. This poetry collection gives voice to these experiences. It is a reflection on the resiliency of the human spirit, the weight of working in the medical field, and the beauty of connection. My hope is that readers come away from these poems with a greater sense of understanding, appreciation, and compassion for others.

A Lesson on How to Live

I learn a lot about life, love, and loss
I'm given advice
More valuable than a
New York Times bestselling book
When I really look
And listen and talk to patients
I discover deep insights
Into the meaning of life
And do you know what they are?
Don't waste this time
You are given
What is your passion
Who do you love
What do you believe
Hold on to these things
And you will live

A life that is fulfilling
It doesn't mean
Things will be easy
There will still be worries
And change
And sorrows and pain
But since we know
We aren't assured tomorrow
Let's live meaningfully today
At least that's what the patients
Who have stared Death right in the face say
So as much as I possibly can
I come home from work
I kiss and hug my children
And I tell them how much
They are loved
Again and again and again

The Midwives of Afghanistan

Learning through telemedicine
Despite a bad internet connection
Living in a conflict zone
Armed with a pencil and a pen
To take notes
A mind full of vision
A heart full of hope
The midwives of Afghanistan
I want to show you
How inspiring they are
Serving their community
Their hunger to learn is evident
By the depth of their questions
As we share from our medical lecture
They say someone died from this condition
How do we stop it from happening again
They are limited
Restricted
But they make a choice to listen
To the suffering of their people
And risk it, act on it

Learn all they can
Even if it's just through telemedicine
And an unstable internet connection
Then they go and implement
Everything we teach them
Travel hours to mountain villages
Everyone matters
They must reach them
Especially the ones with barriers to care
These heroes will go anywhere
My country can learn something here
From these midwives
Who go to the ones who can't come
Who take care of everyone
Even if they're poor
Who would never turn away
A needy patient
Knocking at their door
Heroes of the people
Thank you for what you do
Dear midwives of Afghanistan
We have much to learn from you

Pandemic Heroes

For the ones who saw people die
Right in front of their eyes
For the ones who stayed away
For vulnerable loved ones to be safe
For the ones who put on multiple layers
In hundred-degree weather
Your sacrifice will be remembered

Congratulations

Congratulations on beating cancer
Is my favorite thing to say
Their bright smile at these words
Is the best part of my day
But I know I didn't see
The journey it took to get here
I wasn't there
When they were lying on the bathroom floor
Too weak to get up anymore
I wasn't there through their rounds of
Chemo and radiation
I don't live with that fear of
Did I go through all this
Just to have it return
I don't know what it's like
But I can listen and learn
And as I contemplate the state
Of humanity
Where none of us are guaranteed
A life without sickness and pain
Or watching a loved one suffer
Over and over again
I tell myself

Don't become hardened
Keep your heart open
Always see the best in people
And no matter the darkness
Always let hope in

I'm Sorry I Made You Wait

I'm sorry I made you wait
I see the frustration in your eyes
I hear it in your tone
But I can't tell you what happened
Just moments ago
And I knew we were behind
So instead of taking a minute alone
I came and got you as quickly as I could

You see, what I can't say to you
Is that the patient you were chatting with
Before, in the waiting room
I was the one to scan her
She has unexpected cancer
I was the first to know about it
But had to carry on the conversation
For a bit
Without giving anything away
For I'm not allowed to say
That's the radiologist's job

My heart drops
I already know so much about her
She shares with me stories of
Her small kids and their adventures
I step out of the room
I check in with the doctor
We come back in together
And that's how she finds out she has cancer

I could rush her out
As if we were an assembly line
That's the only way
I could have gotten to you on time

But I gave her some extra moments
To call her husband and cry
I gave her tissues and a hug and said
It's okay if you need more time

I think this is what you would have wanted
If her story would have been yours
I'm sorry I made you wait
I'm done now with your scan
You'll just have to wait
A little bit more

But I know when the doctor
Comes through the door
They'll be giving you good news

I wish I could tell you
To put yourself in my shoes
Every patient will get the best care
From me
But not every patient
Has the same needs
And I can't say all this to you
But in my heart, I know it's true
So though I wish you'd treat me better
You still get my best care
But the patient before you?
I know I'll never forget her

A Sonographer's Workspace

I work out of a dark room
And I love it
I've never been one for
Bright, artificial lights
No, give me darkness
Or real sunshine

The First Heartbeat

Amazement
Wonder
Eyes open wide
The future is bright
"Congratulations on your baby"
I say with a smile
Sometimes they cry
Take each other's hands
Lean in close to one another
Whisper their hopes, dreams, and plans
I step into the background
Where I'm supposed to be
This part of the job
Is always lovely and sweet
There is no sound more
Precious to me
Than the sound of
A baby's first heartbeat

Holding My Breath

I hold my breath
At the start of every first-trimester screening
My body holds a vivid memory
When during my own ultrasound
I learned
My baby was no more
The tech was compassionate and kind
I still remember her gentle eyes
The doctor didn't rush
They both slowed down and made time
For me to take a moment to grieve
They knew that for them
It was another day of work
But for me
It was my life
And the loss of a dream
I was the patient then
Now I am the one to do as they did
When there is devastating news to give
And this is why
I always hold my breath
At the start of this exam

The Fetal Heart

4 chambers
2 atria, 2 ventricles
Knowing where these are is essential
The valves
Tricuspid, mitral, pulmonary, aortic
I write this as a poem for it to stick
In your brain
Next, we have arteries and veins
They carry oxygenated blood
To and away
And don't forget the shunts
They're used to form new pathways
Foramen ovale
Bypasses the lungs
Between the right and left atrium
(I promise this poem is almost done)
But I can't forget to mention
This fact about fetal circulation
Did you know the heart starts beating
At around 5 weeks gestation?
The fetal heart is incredible
Especially the more you know

And when you see it on ultrasound
You'll realize something profound
That something this tiny
Is powerful enough
To keep a baby alive
And I don't know if anything else
Can compare to this design

The Ultrasound Machine

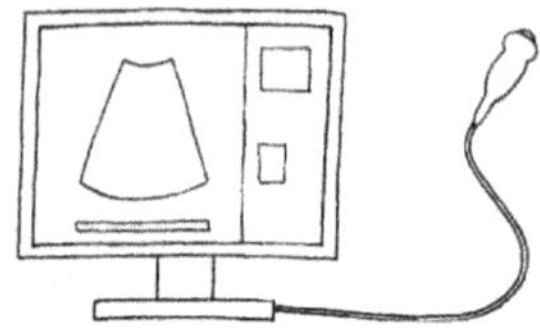

We start and end the day
Together
This job is the perfect balance
Of technology and
Human connection
Fascinating pathology
And clinical investigation
I give focused attention
To all who come before me
I work together with the machine
Our movements are in sync
Together we do extraordinary things
Me and the machine

What Is a Sonographer?

What is a sonographer?
Not to be confused with stenographer
That's a transcriber
And that's not us
You may know us by our other name
Ultrasound technologist
But don't call us technician
Or some techs might see it as a
Disrespect to our profession
See, we don't fix machines
And that's what technician means
But we operate skillfully
We have a mastery
Of anatomy and physiology
And medical terminology
We understand a lot of things
Regarding the human body
And then we have to operate the machine
And for that we utilize physics
We take a special physics exam called the SPI
For this exam, we don't just memorize
We have to know how things work and why
And then we need to apply

Concepts like frequency
Acoustic impedance
And the density of different types of tissue
And be on guard for artifacts
That might show up on screen
But are not real things
We must know how to
Eliminate these illusions
And only image what's reality
And then there are the specialties
Abdomen, OB/GYN, Vascular, Echo
Breast, MSK, Pediatrics, MFM
We take specialty exams
To see if we know
Adequate medical information
Because we are not just picture-takers
We must understand variations
Pathology and labwork
Clinical indications, signs and symptoms
We need to see the big picture
Since we are the eyes of the doctor
Before we can take the specialty exams
We go through formal school
And a clinical training program
Most are for two years

And a lot is crammed into that time
When we are students, it's hard to unwind
Our grades can't drop below a seventy-five
Or we'll be kicked out
And watch our dreams die
After school, we take those specialty exams
The ones I mentioned earlier
Most places won't hire without them
And also 2 years of work
But how to get experience
When you are brand new
It's a difficult thing to do
So as a new grad, we take what we can get
And push through
Often starting out in undesirable situations
Such as
Bad hours, low pay
And a really long commute
But we do what we need to do
To learn and grow
And become the best that we can be
Most of us got into this profession
To help people, you see
(And because we are geeks
About science and technology)

But it's hard times right now
To work in healthcare
Many are burned out
And barely holding on here
Our job pushes us in every way
Mentally, emotionally, and physically
Did you know 90% of sonographers
Scan while in pain?
It's hard on our body
Our cases are sometimes traumatizing
I guess that's why I'm emphasizing
How intense this profession is
Because I do think it's amazing
Stimulating, challenging, and fulfilling
And we're going to need more people joining
But some things need improving
And it starts with understanding
So what is a sonographer?
If you made it to the end
Thanks for listening
Now you know
And with that, I'll go

Student

Late-night studying by a dim light
The baby's asleep
I don't want him to see
How busy I am
So I get less sleep
I drink extra coffee
I study more efficiently
And sometimes this feels like too much
But I'm doing it for him and for us
I'm doing it with love
And that is enough

Clinical Rotations

Student

Will they like me
Will they give me a chance
What if I mess up
What if I look dumb
Do I really have what it takes
To become
Good at this?
I'm so excited to be here
But they look so tired and stressed
I don't want to be a bother
I'm going to give it my best

Preceptor

I wish I had more time to train them
They remind me of my younger self
I know right now they feel overwhelmed
I should say something encouraging
They have so much energy
We could use some of that
We're burned out

Maxed out at capacity
So I don't have much time to spare
But they're the future of healthcare
And we need them here

The Night Shift

Anyone who's ever worked the night shift
Knows the stillness of a world asleep
The humming of a quiet sort of energy
Fluorescent lights flickering
Driving while the streets are empty
You're mostly a zombie
Until the coffee kicks in
Time slows down a little bit
Which is why the night shift
Is some people's preference
It's calm until we're needed
Adrenaline kicks in
And then the work begins

Life as a Humanitarian

Missed a roadside bomb by thirty minutes
On route to the clinic
Not mine but other lives lost
This is something I think about
Quite a lot

War Story

She has aged
In such a beautiful way
But her eyes hold
Memories of sorrow untold
She opens up to me
About her country's history
Families torn apart by war
Her baby, six months old
Separated until she was four
Tears fill her eyes
Because the passing of time
Can't heal everything
She is now seventy-five
And she takes me back
To when she was a scared mother
Missing her child
Longing for her smile
She says
No one should ever kill another
I hate all war and suffering
Tears fill my eyes too
I won't stop thinking about her
I know it will stay with me

Even after I clock out and leave
And that's the thing about this job
It's not just a job
The people and their stories
They have changed me

When Asked About My Day

Sometimes
It is hard to come home
To my family's smiling faces
And be asked about my day
How do I say
It was going well
Until an unexpected third trimester
Fetal demise
And I can't get her screams and cries
Out of my mind
How do I say
We gave her time
As much as we could
Then at some point
We had to move on
And I couldn't explain

Why we were late
To the other patients
I had to bear their frustrations
And give exceptional customer service
While checking to make sure
Their babies were healthy
Which they were
As it looped in my mind, why her?
So sometimes I come home
And I give a one-word answer
I don't mean to hold it in
But then again
Sometimes these things
Are processed better first
With paper and a pen

A Hospital Without Humans

A hospital without humans
Is cold and clinical
Full of beeping sounds and machines
Wires and disease
If it were not for the human touch
Of compassion and comfort
Patients would be scared
If their care
Was systematic
Coming from robots
It would be problematic
Would it not be?
Sure, it might run more efficiently
Since humans need rest
And food and sleep
And a salary
But wouldn't you rather have us
Seeing to your needs
Than something that lacked
Kindness and empathy?
So just remember

Like you, we also bleed
We have hurts and hopes and dreams
Yes, it's our job that we chose
But sometimes the trauma follows us home
And is hard to shake from our bones
We see sickness and fear and death
So many days
And are bombarded with sad stories
And unimaginable pain
So just remember
Like you, we are human
And though our humanity limits us
It is also our greatest strength
And makes us exactly who is meant
To take care of you today

More Than a Job

I've seen both the strength and fragility
Of humanity
I'm with people
On the best and worst
Days of their lives
I've learned things from both
Young and old alike
I've seen how life is not fair
And some are dealt a bad hand
I've marveled as people accept with peace
A path that few could understand
I've seen miracle babies
For those with infertility
Others who never got the miracle
And create a new story
It's more than a job for me
It's a window into
Our shared humanity
And as my paths cross with people
I normally wouldn't meet
I am grateful for the beauty
That I get to see

Opinions

Do you ever think about
Becoming a nurse
They ask me
Do you ever think about
Becoming a doctor
They ask the nurse
If you have kids, how will you balance it
They ask the female doctor
What do you want to be when you grow up
They ask the kid
Let's start doing it this way again
What do you want to be
What do you want to do
Or, tell me more about what it is you do
And friends
Let's be slow to speak
Slow to give our opinion
Genuine in our curiosity
And always quick to listen

Dinner Conversation

This is what you get
Around the dinner table
With a group of healthcare workers
We talk casually about blood and surgery
As we eat, much to the horror
Of an innocent bystander
Who actually has a normal job
But unfortunately for them
Once we get going, we can't stop
So thank you for inviting us
We will be going on in great detail
About disease processes
And bowel and organs
As we eat our portions
Much to the misfortune
Of the innocent bystander
But it truly helps us to unwind
And strangely, this kind of conversation
For us is a good time
To feel understood and seen
Through the chaos we're witnessing
Every single day

So again, I'd like to say
Thank you for the dinner invitation
And the company and the validation
As we swap stories about our jobs
We may be a weird group
But we're also the ones
You'll want in the room
If a medical emergency ever happens to you

Miracles

Miracles exist
Sometimes as unexplained phenomenons
Sometimes through the doctor's wisdom
The steady hands of the surgeon
The nurse's tender compassion
Healthcare workers
Know this tension well
We live in it every day
Where some will heal
And others won't
Lives forever changed
But we'll clock out and go home
To our life that is the same
Until one day
We're the patient
Praying for a miracle
This time
Not as the healer
But as the person
In need of one

A Lesson on How to Live: Part II

To see a person in their thirties
Their body ravaged by disease
It is a sobering thing
I ask about her story
She shares and I am amazed
At the human spirit displayed
So beautifully
With such resiliency
I ask her if there is one thing she wants
People to hear
That she's learned on her journey
From facing her fears of
Her body betraying her
And having to prepare
To leave sooner than she is ready
She says
Be yourself
Don't worry about what they think of you
Live in a way that is brave, kind, and true
I write these words with a sad smile
So that her legacy will live on

Past the passing of time
Time is not her friend
But friends
We should listen
Peace and acceptance
Are hard-fought, hard-won
For her
And although we'd understand if she was
She is not bitter
So step out today
Be yourself
Be brave
At the end of it all
You won't answer to them
At the end
You'll think back to how you lived
Did you live?

When I Am Old

When I am old
And close to the end
Let me go peacefully
Without much intervention
Here in the West
We fear death
And try to delay it
And to be sure
If it is too soon
Then it is a noble thing
To fight against
I myself want to spend my life
Helping end preventable deaths
But if I've lived my life and I'm old
You can let me die
Rather than machines keeping me alive
Let my loved ones be there
Singing songs, saying prayers
Or let me sleep peacefully
Drift off in a dream
When I think about it this way
Death is not as scary
As it may seem

Dear Nurses

I see how you care for
The sick, the hurt, the wounded
Doing the tasks
That few would want to do
I know your feet ache
At the end of every shift
You're mentally exhausted
From being on constant alert
You've been yelled at
Done CPR, saved lives
Watched others die
Sat with the lonely
Comforted grieving families
I see all that you do
And I know this
If there ever was a group of people
Who were angels on Earth
It'd be you

The Heartbeat of Humankind

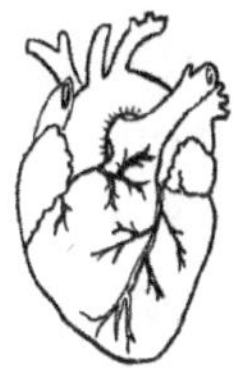

The essence of the human spirit
Lies in the capacity
For love, connection, bravery
Resilience, creativity
A longing to find purpose and meaning
The ability to endure and heal from adversity
To face with courage
Things that are scary
To stand up and say what is true
To do the right thing
Even if no one else is joining
Or even listening
This is the heartbeat
Of humankind
And it is something I find
Over and over again
As I sit with my patients

How Did We Get Here?

Profits over patients
I see it all too clearly
Hurry up with everyone
But treat them better if they're VIP
This is the message
That can come across
From decision-makers
At the top
I'd invite them to come down here
And listen to us share
How we can have what we need
To give our patients the best care
And I'd let them in on a secret
If we are appreciated
And they listen to our perspectives
We'll work like we're not expendable
But with loyalty and motivation
We went into this profession
Because we want to help others
But how can we do that
If the priority is numbers
Profits over patients

How did we get here?
It's a money-making machine
But shouldn't it just be
Healthcare?

I've Seen Too Much

I've seen too much
I may be called idealistic
And unrealistic by some
But it's real, human suffering
That I can't ignore
I won't keep quiet anymore

Money

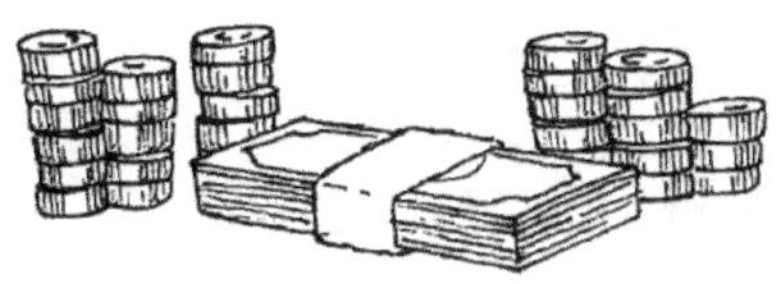

Money is the reason that
Too many
Are not getting
The care that they need
Is money worth
The price of a human life
Let's feed
The corporate greed
Millions
Will line the pockets of the ones above
Let's make sure to turn away
Those who are suffering
Deny them coverage
Cause they can't pay
Now they'll live the rest of their lives
In pain
It's not right
Things are changing

And shifting
The voice of this generation is rising
To say
Healthcare is a human right
And I for one
Am ready to join this fight

Untitled

I was raised to stand up
For what is right
So do not be surprised
When I do

Life as a Humanitarian: Part II

Nothing safe anymore
Roads, schools, hospitals too
People take sides
And they want me to choose
I will always stand against
Loss of innocent life
It doesn't matter to me
Where they are born, live, and die
A humanitarian at heart
I'll gladly cross both sides
Wherever there is suffering
You will see me fight
My weapon is medicine
This is the life of a humanitarian

Imagine

Sometimes I imagine a world
With no sickness and pain
If this were the case
I'd never be so happy
To be unemployed

Sometimes I imagine a world
Without miscarriage, stillbirth, infertility
Every baby born healthy
Every family overjoyed

And then I imagine a world with no death
Or at least, every life fully lived
Drawing our last breath
In old age, a peaceful end

And I look up at the stars and think
We're so small here in this grand universe
Why all these troubles?
Why all this pain?

I wish magic were real
I wish I could touch someone
And they were healed
But the world does not work this way
So I consider my part to play

And I think it is this
I have love and compassion to give
And I'm compelled to spend my life fighting
For more people to live
To see preventable deaths end

And I don't have to imagine
For this to take place
All I have to do
Is live it out today

A Healthcare Worker's Prayer

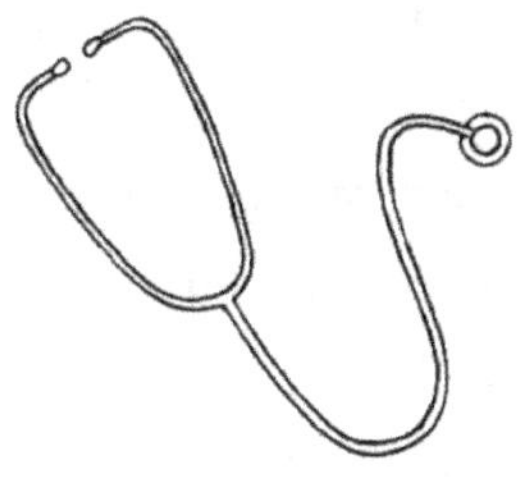

God
Use my hands
To heal and comfort
Make my mind wise
And my words, kind
Let my presence help lessen
Anxiety and fear
So that people in pain
Don't feel so alone here
Give me the strength to face
Whoever you bring
With love and compassion
After all, it's not about me
It's about them and their journey

Their joys and their suffering
So help me not lose sight
That each person is a life
With a whole story behind
And before them
No matter how busy
Let me give them my full attention
Always be happy to listen
Skilled at what I do
Never forgetting the vision
For all to have access
To the care that they need
All, not just the few

www.ingramcontent.com/pod-product-compliance
Lightning Source LLC
LaVergne TN
LVHW021243200726
843509LV00012B/1580